The Journey
Dr. Theresa Scott

All rights reserved. No part of this publication may be reproduced, stored in a retrieval system, or transmitted in any way, by any means – electronic, mechanical, digital, photocopy, recording, or otherwise – without permission of the author, except as provided by the United States of America copyright law.

Copyright © 2019 by Dr. Theresa Scott
Published by Pecan Tree Publishing

Unless otherwise noted, all word definitions are from Merriam-Webster Online Dictionary (www.Merriam-Webster.com), copyright © 2015 by Merriam-Webster, Incorporated. All rights reserved; and Wikipedia [2013], Wikimedia Foundation, Inc. (Wikipedia.org).

Unless otherwise noted, all Scripture quotations are from the King James Version of the Bible.

Scripture quotations marked AMP are from THE AMPLIFIED BIBLE, Old Testament copyright © 1965, 1987 by the Zondervan Corporation. The Amplified New Testament copyright © 1958, 1987 by The Lockman Foundation. Used by permission.

Scripture quotations marked NIV are from the HOLY BIBLE, NEW INTERNATIONAL VERSION. Copyright © 1973, 1978, 1984 by International Bible Society. Used by permission of Zondervan Publishing House. All rights reserved.

Scripture quotations marked MSG are from THE MESSAGE. Copyright © 1993, 1994, 1995. Used by permission of NavPress Publishing Group.

978-1-7347430-4-3 Paperback
978-1-7347430-5-0 Digital
Library of Congress Catalog Number: 2020912322

Cover and Interior Design by: Charlyn Samson

Author Photo Credit:
JAK Visual Arts
www.jonmichal.com
info@jonmichal.com

Pecan Tree Publishing
www.pecantreebooks.com

New Voices | New Styles | New Vision –
Creating a New Legacy of Dynamic Authors and Titles
Hollywood, FL

the journey

DR. THERESA SCOTT

People are Talking...

Dr. Theresa Scott takes us on a most compelling journey, a description of the twists, turns, ups and downs that life will present to us regarding this experience we call *"life."*

As much as we all desire to live a *"perfect life,"* encountering stops, delays or detours are symbolic comparisons explained in this book and are inevitable. In life we are presented with moments when we are mesmerized by love or even blinded to an extent, but the moment revelation causes our eyes to open to the reality of a false sense of love, we find ourselves encountering hate as it arises like the toxic smoke of a smoldering volcano.

Dr. Scott's ability to narrate an explanation as to how the opposites of common emotions or experiences can influence our daily lives and how we make life decisions was extremely intriguing.

One of the most captivating moments was the extracted comparison between **Friend & Foe**. In this chapter you discover the vulnerability of bringing a friend into your life with a heart yielded to 100% trust. The moment the trust meter is decreased by Friend's oppositional behavior, Foe arrives leaving a stain on the relationship.

The Journey is a must read for women from diverse backgrounds or cultures. We all can identify with each twist or turn the journey of life brings our way.

Ayo Thomas
CEO/Founder, Women Own Excellence Magazine (WOE)

In the book, *The Journey*, Dr. Theresa Scott has given us the Cliff Notes to life. Regardless of our ethnicity, nationality, gender, or background, we can all resonate with this book. If you can't, just keep on living. I recommend this book to every young adult because it serves as a warning and gives instructions concerning life. If you are a middle-aged adult, it explains the wrong turns in life. For the mature adult, *The Journey* allows you to reflect, and note the opportunities to make sure you finish strong. *The Journey* is not just a quick read, but it is a *'must'* read.

Anthony Herndon, M.Ed.
District Curriculum Specialist

The Journey is a book that is immensely helpful, convincing, and intriguing. As a 16-year-old, there were many areas I personally related to.. All the chapters were pretty deep. I like how Dr. Scott showed us how people give in too easily, have misconceptions, and suffer in the aftermath. I highly recommend this book for my age group, and even people younger and older than me. *The Journey* did not bore me at all. This book deserves a 10/10 and five stars!

Tamira Campbell

As I began to read *The Journey*, I came across this quote – **"The span of life is your journey."** The key to this quote for me are the words YOUR JOURNEY. Today, people often pattern their lives after someone else's. It can be a parent, older sibling, friend, mentor, etc., mainly because of their success. In doing this, we fail to find the roadmap to our own journey, which causes years of frustration and empty prayers. This selfie generation is captivated by highlights of someone's life via social media, but do not realize this is not the sum of one's life journey. It is only a snapshot of one moment in time.

As you take this journey through life, know your Road Buddies, and put them in their proper place. They are not your end. They are the beginning of a fulfilled life. Use them as tools of reflection and teachable moments in your passage through life. Thank you Dr. Theresa Scott for this compass.

Kesha Cook, B.S.
Dean of Students, High School

The Journey resonated with me. This book talked about some things my generation (Generation Z) has problems with when it comes to relationships. In the chapter **Love & Hate**, I like the way Dr. Scott addressed how sometimes people are so in love that they dismiss all the negatives. In my generation this happens a lot because people are so caught up on what the person can provide for them, and how they make them feel. It's nothing wrong with that; but love is not just about a feeling. When the feeling changes and we don't work out differences, that opens the door for hate. She also pointed out how, after arguing so much, love turned on us and left us in a state of hatred.

I also enjoyed the chapters on **Friend & Foe** as well as **Success & Failure**. Both chapters talked about taking risks, enjoying the process, and knowing what people to involve in your life. With my generation, everyone wants to call each other 'friends', but they are around all the failures and don't realize it. When success comes, you must start removing some of those failures because you can't take them into the next chapter of your life. When you do this, they become a foe because they want you to feel like they are more successful. Once you make that decision to remove them, they now want to talk bad about you and throw dirt on your name.

The Journey really explains the realities, **Road Buddies**, in our lives. All we have to do is to take the advice given in the Lessons Learned. This will help to make my generation wiser and not just well-informed.

Jasiah Scott
CEO/Founder, After the Ball Deflates, LLC

Contents

Foreword v
People are Talking vii
Acknowledgements xv
Dedication xvii
Introduction xix
The Journey 1
The Road Buddies 3
    1. Love & Hate 5
    2. Trust & Betrayal 14
    3. Friend & Foe 22
    4. Happy & Sad 30
Rest Stop 38
    5. Courage & Fear 40
    6. Success & Failure 48
    7. Rich & Poor 56
    8. Well & Sick 64
    9. Truth & Lies 72
Rescued 80
The Making Process 82
In Retrospect 85
About the Author 87

Acknowledgements

What started out as a presentation at a women's conference in 2012 has ended up in book form – **The Journey**. I am grateful to the many people who have struggled in relationships, that I counseled and ministered to over the years. Many were naïve and found themselves clueless in the unpredictable behavior of others. With the help of God and your inner strength, you overcame relational devastation and got back into the arena of life.

I am thankful for the tremendous amount of encouragement from and dialogue with my adult children and grandchildren.

I would be remiss in not acknowledging my husband, Richard Levi Scott, who gently nudged me along to complete this project. He is the wind beneath my wings.

Most importantly, I am grateful to God for pulling all of this together after so many years. He knows what's needed in our 'now' seasons of life.

Dedication

The Journey is dedicated to Teenagers, Millennials, Generation-X, Generation-Z, and Baby Boomers. It is for those who ignore the warning signs of life. It is for those who have relational trust issues. It is for those who continually seek the validation and affirmation of others. It is for those who are clueless and naïve about life.

I hope ***The Journey*** will encourage you to continue your life's Journey despite your encounters with the **Road Buddies.** Don't allow them to sabotage the maturing process in your life.

Introduction

I was inspired to write this book to let people know that life is not always going to be a bowl of cherries. Once we get a better idea of what's involved, the better we can handle it. This minimizes some of the long term woes, murmurings, and complaints. Life is full of crazies. You experience sorrow, disappointment, abandonment, depression, etc. However, you should not allow the negatives to define you. To the contrary, you also experience joy, genuine love, happiness, and peace. What you dwell on (think about) determines your outcome. I'm not telling you to be delusional or ignore the realities in your life. I'm telling you to learn from those experiences in order to make your life better and not bitter.

Life is a Journey. The Journey is how you live it – the in-between of the beginning and the end of your destination. At this in-between stage you are going to meet up with what I call **Road Buddies**. These **Road Buddies** are the realities of life. All of us are acquainted with them. They are the good and bad experiences we inevitably encounter.

This book is dedicated to Teenagers, Millennials, Generation-X, Generation-Z, and Baby Boomers. It is for those who ignore the warning signs of life. It is for those who have relational trust issues.

DR. THERESA SCOTT

It is for those who continually seek the validation and affirmation of others. It is for those who are naïve about life.

I hope *The Journey* will encourage you to continue on your life's Journey in spite of your encounters with the **Road Buddies**. Don't allow them to knock you out of the arena of life.

Dr. Theresa Scott

The Journey

"Better is the end of a thing than the beginning."
(Ecclesiastes 7:8)

Life is a Journey filled with all sorts of events, circumstances, and experiences – good and bad.

We didn't have the privilege of choosing how our Journey began. We didn't get to choose our parents, the family we grew up in, or where we grew up. All we know for sure is that we are here. The true realities and purpose in life become all the more meaningful when we give our lives to Christ – become born-again. Surrendering a life to Him enables one to discover their true identity and purpose. In Christ you can experience inner joy, peace and fulfillment in any given situation. He takes the sting out of a dysfunctional upbringing.

As we move along on our Journey, we discover life has a way of teaching us some valuable lessons. *Note: Our Journey would be easier if we follow the wise counsel given to us along the way.*

A *journey* is defined as a distance traveled in a specified time. It is going from one place to another especially a long distance. The span of life is your Journey

The Road Buddies

Let's set the stage before embarking on this Journey. In life's Journey you either walk by yourself or with someone. You are a tri-part being – spirit, soul and body. You have ways of conversing with yourself via thoughts, words, and actions. You entertain your thoughts as they express your inner self. Then you talk to yourself. When talking to yourself you articulate those thoughts. Hearing yourself talk brings clarity to a situation. After the thinking and self-talk, you take action. Needless to say you are really a *'we'* – spirit, soul and body. Yet you are one person.

When you walk with someone in your life you acknowledge their ways as well as your own. You get feedback from them. Therefore, we have a physical *'we'* on our Journey. I reference the Journey with two people walking and collaborating together – *'we.'* I purposely did this because inevitably you are never totally alone on your Journey. Your Journey involves you and someone else. The *'we'* in this book refers to two people experiencing the same encounters together.

On our Journey we meet some **Road Buddies – Love & Hate, Rich & Poor, Well & Sick, Happy & Sad, Truth & Lies, Friend & Foe, Success & Failure, Trust & Betrayal,** and **Courage & Fear.** Even though they are opposites, they travel in pairs. They don't necessarily walk side by side. They have a very unique way of distancing themselves. In addition, they have subtle ways of revealing themselves. If you aren't careful and don't pay attention, they will catch you by surprise. Let me introduce them to you.

1. Love & Hate

While walking along our Journey, it seems as if something is lacking within us. It's a craving we can't adequately describe. It's like we want to be cared for, validated, affirmed or noticed. Actually some affection would be welcomed as well. No sooner than us talking about this, **Love** walks up beside us.

Let's get an understanding of what *love* is. The English word *love* can refer to a variety of different feelings, states, and attitudes ranging from interpersonal affection to pleasure. It can refer to an emotion of a strong attraction and personal attachment.

In terms of interpersonal attraction, four forms of *love* have traditionally been distinguished, based on ancient Greek precedent, as – *storge* (love of kinship or familiarity), *philia* (love of friendship), *eros* (love of sexual or romantic desire), and *agape* (self-emptying or divine love). *Storge* is natural love. *Philia* is love of the mind. *Eros* is love of the body. *Agape* is love of the soul.

Love is an assurance of affection. The Urban Dictionary blog says *"love is giving someone the power to destroy you, and trusting them not to.*" For our purpose we're using this latter definition.

So here is **Love**. Oh my, he's talking good. We engage in some light conversations. Our neediness leads us into more in-depth conversations about ourselves. We open up to him. We talk about our longings and desires. Wow! It's like he knows what we want. He understands our passionate feelings of needing to be understood and loved. He said he could make us feel real good through other people, and things like money, food and position. Hey! We need something. What the heck? Let's try it. We experienced pleasure after pleasure. The love, romance, affection and sex lit us up. This is exactly what we've been looking for. The validations and promises of care and protection drew us in all the more. He was talking real good. We knew we belonged to him and nobody else. We're okay with that. Why would we need anyone else anyway?

After a period of time we noticed some issues of control. We dismissed it because we were convinced he really loved us. Then all of a sudden **Love** turned on us. How could **Love** do this to us after we were having such a good time? After all we were *"in love"* or so we thought. We found ourselves arguing a lot. It was like the battle of the wills. We tried to change each other, but that was futile. Attitudes and tones of voices became disrespectful and harsh. Tempers kept flaring up. We were on an emotional roller coaster of highs and lows. We began to dislike each other more and more. That dislike led to outright hate. We hated ourselves and we hated him. **Love** took off the mask. **Hate** was revealed.

Hate or *hatred* is a deep and emotional extreme dislike that can be directed against individuals, entities, objects or ideas. *Hatred* is often associated with feelings of anger and a disposition towards hostility.

Sigmund Freud (Founder of Psychoanalysis) defined *hate* as an ego state that wishes to destroy the source of its unhappiness. The Penguin Dictionary of Psychology defines *hate* as a deep, enduring, intense emotion expressing animosity, anger, and hostility towards a person, group or object. *Hatred* is believed to be long-lasting. Many psychologists consider it to be more of an attitude or disposition than a temporary emotional state.

The very thing we thought we loved, now we *hate*. We had no idea **Love** and **Hate** were **Road Buddies**. We thought they were opposites, and in fact they are. However, where one left off, the other picked up. It's mind-boggling how on one hand we so quickly and passionately fell in love, and on the other hand hated with a vengeance.

As a result, we suffered deep heartache. Our passion blinded us. It was lust, not love. Our insecurities left us vulnerable. We need a time-out after all of this drama!!

Lesson Learned

Love and Hate are strong emotions. No matter what type of love you experience you take a risk. It is a good risk coming from the sincerity of your heart. Do not allow bad experiences to hinder the flow of love that emanates from you. Learn from each experience as to how far you allow love to take you. Guard your heart by using discernment.

Persistent hate is detrimental to your well-being. If you don't let it go after a period of time, it can cause mental and physical sickness. Hate requires a lot of mental energy that leaves you drained. The reason for the hate may be justifiable, but do everything in your power to send it back from where it originated. Release it from you. It's not worth it.

"Hate leaves ugly scars; love leaves beautiful ones."
(Mignon McLaughlin, Author)

What Love taught me....

THE JOURNEY

DR. THERESA SCOTT

What Hate taught me....

THE JOURNEY

2. Trust & Betrayal

We were devastated by **Love & Hate**. It took a long while, but we're better. As we travel on our Journey trying to keep our heads clear, we meet **Trust**. We are a little leery about him. **Love & Hate** left us with some major trust issues.

Trust means to place confidence in. It is an assured reliance on the character, ability, strength or truth of someone or something – one in which confidence is placed.

We didn't say too much to **Trust**. We just let him talk. We kept checking him out and listening. We got to know him. After a period of time we told **Trust** what **Love & Hate** did to us. He understood, but told us not to judge every relationship like that. He kept saying *"you can **trust** me."* He said he wasn't like the others. We thought *"yeah, right – we'll see."* By and by we opened up to **Trust** – actually we were still needy. We didn't keep discerning the relationship because we felt we did our homework. We didn't want to be defined by misconceived **Love** and the bitterness of **Hate**.

However, unbeknown to us, we weren't completely healed from **Love & Hate**. We still had validation issues and low self-esteem. Nevertheless, we decided to give **Trust** a try.

Trust kept his word. He did everything he could for us to believe in him. He wasn't perfect. He would slip up ever so often, but had valid reasons for it.

As time went on **Trust** kept coming up with excuses for not keeping his word. He would say one thing but do the opposite. Something was not right!! Little by little **Trust's** appearance started changing. He wasn't looking right. **Trust** had been camouflaging **Betrayal**. By the time we realized it **Betrayal** slammed **Trust**.

Betrayal means to lead astray – seduce. It means to fail or desert especially in time of need. It also means to disclose in violation of confidence. Synonyms for *betrayal* – backstab, cross, double-cross, two-time!!

Betrayal stepped out and took over **Trust**. See, we should have put the brakes on **Trust** when his behavior kept being raggedy. He couldn't stay true to his word. Now here's **Betrayal**. Everything we told **Trust** in confidence, **Betrayal** took it and turned it against us. More drama! **Betrayal** played us over and over again. He knocked us down, jerked our emotions around, and threw us under the bus. We got to get up from here!

Lesson Learned

Trust is trial and error. Trust has to be earned and proven. Trust takes time. You learn to trust as you develop a relationship. During this time of development take note of what can and cannot be trusted or kept in confidence.

Betrayal is a stinger. It catches you by surprise. Oftentimes betrayal stems from another person being jealous of you. They act out their inadequacies.

> *"Everyone suffers at least one bad betrayal in*
> *their lifetime. It's what unites us.*
> *The trick is not to let it destroy your trust*
> *in others when that happens.*
> *Don't let them take that from you."*
> (Sherrilyn Kenyon, Writer)

DR. THERESA SCOTT

What Trust taught me....

THE JOURNEY

What Betrayal taught me....

THE JOURNEY

3. Friend & Foe

We're feeling pretty isolated on our Journey. The terrain on this Journey thus far has been rugged. We just need to walk some things out. Right now no more intimate relationships. We don't want to talk about the past events. It hurts too much. But after a while this inner dialogue gets old. It seems like we're not much help to each other. It sure would be nice if we could connect with a genuine friend. Nothing intimate – just a friend to dialogue with. Lo and behold we walk up to this person. She is quite friendly and polite. Her name is **Friend**.

So what is a *friend*? A *friend* is a favored companion. It is one that favors or promotes something. It is one who is not hostile. Synonyms for **friend** are amigo, buddy, comrade, confidant, pal. Characteristics of a *friend* are loyalty, intelligence, sensitivity, humor, honesty, listening, supportive, and generous.

After all we've been through we talk cautiously to **Friend**. We tread lightly – not giving up too much personal info. **Friend** seems cool. Light conversations at first. Then we talked about similar likes and dislikes. We discover that we are from the same state. After knowing **Friend** for some time she seemed supportive – always giving a listening ear. She is business savvy and gave us some sound business advice. We loved **Friend's** sense of humor. It was good to laugh again – feel safe.

When we first saw **Friend**, we also saw a flash of someone behind **Friend**, but dismissed it. **Friend** was always encouraging us and concerned about our welfare. We were having some good times together.

After a while **Friend** began to change. She became authoritative. Everything had to be her way or no way. Now everything was about her and what she was doing. She stopped being supportive of us. Here we go again – flash backs! The things we confided in **Friend** was being used against us. She said we were weak, dumb, stupid, ignorant and insecure. Immediately **Foe** came to the forefront.

What is a *foe*? A *foe* is one who has personal enmity for another. It is an adversary or opponent. Some synonyms for *foe* are enemy, antagonist, rival, ill-wisher.

Well, **Foe** took over. Blew everything out of proportion that we told **Friend**. **Foe** was hostile. She started to act like **Hate** – dah!! **Foe** fought us tooth and nail on everything we said and wanted to do. She actually spoke word curses over us. Wait a minute sista! We may not have your expertise, but the buck stops here and NOW!!

Lesson Learned

Like trust, friendship has to be earned. Don't tell a friend everything. Come to know the purpose of friendships. There are many types of friendships – best friends, childhood friends, business friends, work friends, church friends, girlfriends, boyfriends, etc. All of which are to be treated differently and should only be opened up to accordingly.

Each friend should have a boundary in your life. Boundaries are like fences with gates. The fences protect the property. The gates open and shut. You control who you let in and who you keep out. Come to grips with the fact that you are not going to be liked by everyone. People can dislike you for no justifiable reason. That's their problem, not yours.

> *"Nobody sees a flower really; it is so small. We haven't time, and to see takes time – like to have a friend takes time."*
> (Georgia O'Keeffe, Artist)

DR. THERESA SCOTT

What Friend taught me....

THE JOURNEY

4. Happy & Sad

Life has really been teaching us some major lessons on this Journey. We've had enough of crazy relationships. We just want to be happy. We decided we're gonna make ourselves happy. But don't we need something to happen in order to be happy? What can make us happy? We want some happy experiences. Food makes us happy. New clothes makes us happy. Driving a nice car is a good happy. Perhaps we should socialize at a Happy Hour – meet new people. Drink and laugh. Yeah, but the *ultimate* happy is some good ole banging sex!!

Happy – enjoying or characterized by well-being and contentment. It is enjoying or showing marked pleasure.

We found **Happy**. **Happy** gave us some good times and lots of fun. **Happy** was a taskmaster - working us hard with so many demands. **Happy** is expensive too – taking all our money. **Happy** got us in some major debt. We realized we didn't have the wherewithal to keep this up. It was like being on a perpetual high that has to be sustained. **Happy** was never satisfied – in fact, thrived on short term gratification. Regardless of how bad it is, we got to keep **Happy** going.

Can't let **Happy** go. It's like an addiction we can't shake. We have become **Happy** junkies! Then this woman named **Sad** appeared out of nowhere.

Sad – affected with or expressive of grief or unhappiness – depressing. It causes sorrow or regret. It is deplorably bad. *Sadness* is emotional pain associated with or characterized by feelings of loss, disadvantage, despair and helplessness. *Sad* aka (also known as) blue, brokenhearted, cast down, dejected, depressed, despondent, gloomy, heartsick, miserable.

Sad came and found us at the lowest point of our lives. **Sad** kept reminding us over and over about the mess we got ourselves in trying to be **Happy**. She said the reality is we were never meant to be happy. We should be ashamed of ourselves. Nobody has a happy life. They look happy; but they are not. She said **Happy** is a fake. OMG! **Sad** beat us up day and night with depression, guilt and condemnation. **Sad** is a tormentor straight from hell. Whatever we experienced with **Happy** she destroyed. **Sad** annihilated the remembrance of our **Happy** moments. **Sad** was mean. She was a kill joy. **Sad** near 'bout left us in a suicidal state.

Lesson Learned

THE JOURNEY

DR. THERESA SCOTT

What Sad taught me....

THE JOURNEY

Rest Stop

Break time on this Journey. What have we learned thus far? We got to take time to reflect on these past experiences. These **Road Buddies** have been fierce. They've been teaching us some hard life lessons.

Love & Hate – We put a lot into **Love**. We gave it our all. We were so needy – just wanted somebody to give us some love and affection. We wanted it at any cost. As a result, we were blinded by its negative overtones which opened the door for **Hate**. We didn't think we had it in us to hate with such a passion. This encounter really hurt. The heartache was devastating. We learned the difference between love and lust. Lust was like an instant gratification that soon wore off. Love is to be a good and genuine experience. We just needed to give it some time. We realized we needed to love and accept ourselves *first* before expecting to receive it from someone else.

Trust & Betrayal – It took almost a year for us to recover from **Love & Hate**. We got a little paranoid about relationships after that. However, we licked our wounds and met **Trust**. We took our time, but got anxious again. We eventually learned that **Trust** and **Love** takes time. We knew there was an inner witness we didn't pay attention to. We never thought we could be so viciously betrayed by someone. Being betrayed by someone you trust really cut us deep. It's like bad things happening to good people. The betrayal was not our fault, and we will not take the blame for it. We had to get that off of us.

Friend & Foe – **Foe** was very belligerent. The *cussing* and hate was ridiculous. We wanted to fight her bad. She needed a beat-down. However, looking back she wasn't worth a fight. We had to leave her to herself – her crazy self. We now know that everybody we meet will not be our friend no matter how friendly they are. Some people are only associates for a season of time. It's nothing wrong with having friends because we need them. Just know the purpose of the friendship.

Happy & Sad – Wow! Wow! Wow! These two **Road Buddies** did us in. We really don't want to talk about them too much because what they did to us still hurts. This healing is going to take some time. These two afflicted our souls. We experienced super highs and detrimental lows. We can never, ever afford to open ourselves up to encounters like that again. Nothing was wrong with **Happy**. **Happy** was good. We had fun. However, we let **Happy** get out of control. What made us think we could live like that *all* the time? Then those dark experiences with **Sad**. We know everybody experiences sadness. We just didn't realize the depths of sadness. We gave **Sad** too much place. We didn't have sense enough to put **Sad** out. We allowed **Happy & Sad** to control our emotions. Looking back, we see how dangerous it is to be governed by your emotions *all* the time.

5. Courage & Fear

We've gotten a little older – had a few birthdays. Hopefully we've put away some immature ways. Time to grow up. We talk among ourselves and **Journey** on. We need to make some lifestyle changes. Here comes **Courage** running toward us.

Courage is defined as mental or moral strength to venture, persevere and withstand danger, fear or difficulty. Physical courage is courage in the face of physical pain, hardship, death or threat of death. Moral courage is the ability to act rightly in the face of popular opposition, shame, scandal or discouragement.

We don't do well with sudden approaches. This person comes straight at us. He introduced himself – **Courage**. **Courage** says he's been looking for us for a long time. He's been asking if anyone has seen us. Word on the street, he says, is that we were beaten up pretty bad by **Sad**, **Foe** and **Betrayal**. He was hoping he would find us alive. That's why he was so glad to catch up with us. **Courage** is bold and positive. He said our lives are not over because of the past. He quickly encouraged us and told us we could do whatever we set our minds to. He's so upbeat. **Courage** told s us how we can face our adversities and overcome them. He's a cheerleader.

Courage told us to believe in ourselves – there's good in us. He motivated us to change the way we think – think up not down! **Courage** raised our self-esteem. We felt life come into us. **Courage** woke us up to hope. *Okay*, we said, *we can do it*. As soon as we got our minds together, here comes this person charging at **Courage**. It's **Fear** aka **What If**.

Fear is defined as frighten; to be afraid or apprehensive. Synonyms for *fear* are worry, stress, trouble. Common fears – fear of death (when, where and how), fear of the unknown (uncertainty), fear of survival (how will we make it?), and unpredictability (unpredictable environment leading to anxiety).

Fear attacked everything **Courage** said we could do. While **Fear** was attacking **Courage** we remembered what **Courage** told us. We didn't like what **Fear** was saying. Our minds had been changed for the better. Our lives had hope because of **Courage**. We told **Fear** to back off of **Courage**. **Fear** kept shouting over and over *'what if'*. However, this time we were not listening. Enough already!! We told **Fear** to shut up. He had no place in our lives. We are fully persuaded that **everything Courage** told us is true and we **can** do it.

Lesson Learned

Courage faces fear and moves on anyhow. Courage begins with a state of mind. It is a psychological strength. It entails being brave and persevering. If you can think it and believe it, you can do it. To be courageous is to be relentless. You have to *do* in spite of the challenge. Realize this is not going to be the death of you.

Don't allow fear to immobilize you. Remember fear will always try to convince you of something that has yet to happen. Fear relates to future events such as the worsening of a bad situation or the continuation of it being unacceptable. Work on a process to neutralize the effects of fear. Ernest Hemingway (American Writer) famously defined *courage* as *'grace under pressure.'*

"We don't develop courage by being happy every day. We develop it by surviving difficult times and challenging adversity."
(Barbara De Angelis, Author, Relationship Consultant)

DR. THERESA SCOTT

What Courage taught me....

THE JOURNEY

What Fear taught me....

THE JOURNEY

6. Success & Failure

Thanks to **Courage**, we're doing rather good on this Journey. Life is looking much better. We're experiencing confidence. We've been talking about what we want to do in life. Well, well, well! Who is this? None other than **Success**. *It's such an honor and pleasure to meet you. We've heard a lot about you. We understand you help people fulfill their dreams.* **Success** talks to us about our purpose – what we want to do in life. He then begins giving us strategies and ideas. This is exactly what we need. We start setting goals and executing plans. This time we're paying attention. We are following advice. We're getting some immediate results from **Success**. Wow, it's so good to get solid counsel – counsel that produces. **Success** is working. It's genuine.

Success is a favorable or desired outcome. To *succeed* means to turn out well; to attain a desired object or end.

Uh oh – what now? Looks like **Success** is falling apart. What's going on? We had our plans. Did our homework. Counted the cost. We experienced **Success**. Now it seems some things are not working out as planned. What are these unforeseen circumstances **Success** didn't tell us about? We're going down and have landed on **Failure**.

Failure – a state of inability to perform. It is the lack of success; falling short. It also means to lose strength. *Failure* is the state or condition of not meeting a desirable or intended objective.

We didn't plan for **Failure**. That was not in the equation. Thomas J. Watson (American Businessman) is attributed with saying *"If you want to succeed, double your failure."* A situation considered to be a failure by one might be considered a success by another.

Failure hit us hard. We were at the door of depression trying to open it. Somehow we remembered how **Courage** was looking for us and what he told us. We had to re-group and pick ourselves up. We walked away from depression. We got our minds together and kicked **Failure** to the curb! We're going to keep at it until **Success** shows up. We will succeed!

Lesson Learned

THE JOURNEY

DR. THERESA SCOTT

What Failure taught me....

THE JOURNEY

7. Rich & Poor

This Journey is sweet now. We got more than enough. No lack here. We're living the high life. We've come up in life because we deserve it. **Rich** is here. He told us we are supposed to be **rich** after all we've been through. That's right! We worked hard for this. We almost died getting to this place. It's all about us now. We can buy what we want. Live where we want. Go where we want. We don't need nothing from nobody. Goodbye Wal-Mart, Goodwill and Salvation Army. Goodbye Chevy, Ford and Honda. Spend, spend, spend!! Look at all these credit cards we qualify for. We must have pretty good credit. We max out one card and get another one. All we have to do is make minimum payments. Who cares – we're living for the moment.

To be *rich* is having abundant possessions, especially material wealth. It is high value or quality. It is magnificently impressive.

There's nothing wrong in being rich. We and **Rich** are living for the moment. Tomorrow will take care of itself!!!! Right??

We were staying on top of the latest economic news – checking stocks and bonds daily. But suddenly the economy crashed.

The dollar lost its value. Companies were downsizing with lay-offs. Gas prices were skyrocketing. Houses were losing their market value or going into foreclosure. We invested in a retirement plan and thought we would be able to get some money out of that. When we tried to contact them we were told there was no money in our account. The company was bankrupt! We found ourselves going from **Rich** to **Poor** in a moment.

Poor is a state of poverty; lacking material possessions. It is less than adequate. It's small in worth and inferior in quality or value. It is lacking a normal or adequate supply of something. *Poor* is a spirit that draws you into lack mentally and physically.

Poor began to mock us. He called us fools!! **Poor** said because we didn't know the purpose of riches we abused it and that's how he showed up. **Poor** reminded us of our selfishness. He said he was a spirit sent to us to force us into lack and poverty. Both affecting the way we think. **Poor** made us feel inferior. **Poor** lowered our self-esteem and self-worth. What were we going to do? We had nothing. We started remembering somewhere on our Journey that when you don't know the purpose of a thing you will abuse it. We didn't understand the real purpose of **Rich**. We didn't know how to handle sudden wealth. We actually trusted in our riches.

Lesson Learned

We are blessed to be a blessing. Learn to live beyond the moment in the midst of abundance. You control money. Don't let money control you.

Riches can be fleeting if you don't manage it properly. Riches come in various forms. Therefore, don't always restrict it to material possessions. You can be rich in character. Rich in relationships. Rich in knowledge and in certain skill-sets.

Poor symbolizes lack and inadequacies. This can be internal as well as external. Poor thoughts produce a poor lifestyle. How you think is how you act. How you act is how you live.

> *"Your future is created by what you do today, not tomorrow."*
> (Robert Kiyosaki, American Businessman)

DR. THERESA SCOTT

What Rich taught me....

What Poor taught me....

THE JOURNEY

8. Well & Sick

Moving right along. **Well** walks with us. He lets us know we're looking pretty good physically. We told him we have no aches or pains. We eat any and everything. We may have occasional indigestion or constipation, but we get OTC (over-the-counter) meds and that takes care of it. We may put our bodies through some stress and strain, but we always bounce back. That's a part of life. We're feeling invincible. No need of a doctor because we're healthy. We heard going to the doctor annually is preventative care, but we don't need him to tell us we're okay. We can save that money. If there is a problem, we can always go to the pharmacist and get another OTC med. We got our health under control. **Well** did ask us about exercising. But all this walking we've been doing on this Journey, we're in decent shape. It seemed like **Well** wanted to talk some more about our health, but hesitated because we had an answer for everything. So **Well** let it go.

Well is simply being healthy. It is being in a satisfactory condition.

We've been walking on this Journey for a very long time now – gotten a little older, but not old. For some reason we started feeling unexplainable lumps and knots on our bodies. We tend to get tired a lot. Sometimes our vision gets blurred. We may need some reading glasses. There are other things going on as well. Why is our urine real yellow, heart racing? What's with the persistent dizziness, loss of appetite, difficulty breathing, and gaining weight for no reason? Why can't we shake a cold? What's happening to us? Didn't **Well** say we had our health under control? We felt so bad that we had to sit down on the side of the road. Who is this? "Hey. I'm **Sick**."

Sick is being afflicted with a disease or ill health. It is lacking vigor. It is also mentally or emotionally unsound or disordered.

Sick was very tall. He stood over us and gave us a long look. **Sick** told us our body had been talking to us but we weren't listening. What are you talking about? We didn't know the body could talk! **Sick** said the body talks to us by way of aches, pains and discomforts. These are signs that something is wrong with us. **Sick** further explained if we had annual check-ups with the doctor some of these ailments could have been dealt with sooner. **Sick** said *"you're **sick** – really **sick**."* He said for the most part we made our own selves **sick**. He didn't say anything after that. **Sick** just stood there looking at us while our bodies were screaming for help. We got to pause for a while on this Journey – got to go to the doctor!!!!

Lesson Learned

Don't take your health for granted, listen to your body. Taking care of your body not only benefits you, but others around you. When you become negligent you inevitably put a burden on others to care for you. Bad health is expensive. A healthy body can keep some money in the bank!

> *"Health is not valued till sickness comes."*
> (Thomas Fuller, Historian)

DR. THERESA SCOTT

What Well taught me....

THE JOURNEY

What Sick taught me....

THE JOURNEY

9. Truth & Lies

Looks like we're approaching the end of our Journey. As we reflect on it, we remember what we've learned from the **Road Buddies** we encountered. They were a trip. Some tried to kill us – preventing us from getting to the end of our Journey. Then others came to ensure we made it. However, they all taught us some priceless lessons. We had to experience all of them. Each **Road Buddy** made us better.

On this last leg we encounter **Truth & Lies**. They didn't come disguised. They are who they are. This is a little strange because they walk side by side. **Truth** tells us what we really don't want to hear but know deep down it's right. Some of what **Truth** told us hurt. We had to own up to it; and when we did it freed us up. Truth changed our perception about ourselves, other people, and life in general.

Truth is sincerity in action, character and utterance. *Truth* is the body of real things, events and facts – actuality.

Lies stroke our ego, tickle our ears and tell us what we want to hear. It's very appealing in its deception. *Lies* mislead or deceive. It is an assertion of something known or believed by the speaker to be untrue with the intent to deceive. A *lie* is a false statement.

Truth & Lies said they would always be around us – talking to us. It will always be up to us which one we listen to. They told us to consider the consequences of what they say. Always get the facts!

Truth said it will take life's experiences for us to discern and be fully persuaded that what he tells us is right. He comes with good consequences. **Truth** warns us to think – discern. **Lies** said he will always make us feel good, but remember he comes with dire consequences. **Lies** also said he will tell us a half-truth!!

Lesson Learned

Truth is liberating yet hard to accept at times. Strive to live a truthful life. Be true to yourself. Accept the truths about you. This avoids being so defensive in relationships. Come to grips with the fact that everyone is not going to be as truthful as you are.

Every individual has lied or will lie. You cannot escape being lied to. Stop allowing lies to shut you down. You may be taken by surprise by who lied to you, but it's not the end of the world. As long as you know the truth, be secure in that. A lie is a lie. Truth will *prevail*.

> *"Truth has a power only the courageous can handle."*
> (Anthon St Maarten, Destiny Consultant)

What Truth taught me....

THE JOURNEY

DR. THERESA SCOTT

What Lies taught me....

THE JOURNEY

Rescued

After a period of time, we acknowledged our shortcomings on this Journey. Life's experiences have a way of showing us who we really are. We come to realize we are capable of doing some unlikely things based on who and what we've given place to.

We continue on our Journey. We embark upon some rugged terrain. There are *mountains too high to climb, valleys too low to cross, waters too high to swim, winds too strong to bear, deserts too dry to endure, decisions too hard to make.*

We do what we can to make it. Our decisions can leave us with some life-threatening consequences. Some consequences are so detrimental we medicate ourselves with drugs, get involved in toxic relationships, become workaholics, or sell our souls for a brief moment of satisfaction.

It's these things we encounter on life's Journey that let us know we need help and can't travel it by ourselves.

After a long period of time, we become so exhausted and worn out, that we can't go on. Then a man shows up and introduces Himself as **Jesus Christ**. He said He came to help – lighten our load. He offers us a new life. He gives us comfort and healing. He seems to know all about us. **Jesus** tells us His way is the best way on this Journey. As He speaks He makes

THE JOURNEY

Jesus told Peter that Satan was behind **Denial**. Satan wanted to sift him like wheat. Jesus had already prayed that Peter's faith would not fail. Jesus prayed that Peter would get himself together and keep believing what Jesus taught him. **Denial** was trying to drag Peter back to **Lies**, but Jesus intervened. **Truth** prevailed. The **Spirit of Truth** came and knocked **Denial** off the road of Peter's Journey. It strengthened Peter's faith and loyalty to Christ

You've come too far on your Journey to stop now. Don't quit because of the rugged terrain. Don't get sidetracked by the chatter of the **Road Buddies**. You are going to make it through your Journey.

In the Book of Revelations, Jesus told the church in Philadelphia -

> *I see what you've done. Now see what I've done. I've opened a door before you that no one can slam shut. You don't have much strength, I know that; you used what you had to keep my Word. You didn't deny me when times were rough. And watch as I take those who call themselves true believers but are nothing of the kind, pretenders whose true membership is in the club of Satan – watch as I strip off their pretensions and they're forced to acknowledge it's you that I've loved. Because you kept my Word in passionate patience, I'll keep you safe in the time of testing that will be here soon, and all over the earth, every man, woman, and child put to the test. I'm on my way; I'll be there soon. KEEP A TIGHT GRIP ON WHAT YOU HAVE SO NO ONE DISTRACTS YOU AND STEALS YOUR CROWN.* (Revelations 3:8-11, MSG)

Don't let other people's twisted views and philosophical conceptions of your Journey cause you to lose your way. Keep God's Word. Don't deny His name. Don't let no man take your crown. Remember you'll live in eternity longer than you'll live on this earth.

"Better is the end of a thing than the beginning."
(Ecclesiastes 7:8)

In Retrospect

At various junctures in life I take time to reflect where I've been, where I am now and where I'm going. I look at where I've been as something positive. I don't view my liabilities as the worse things that happened to me. I view them as learning curves. In reflecting back I'm not trying to connect with some negative energy. Rather I'm looking at what caused it and my mindset at the time. I find I was experiencing some *age appropriate* activities that lacked wise decision-making. We mature at different levels in life.

When I examine me, I do so objectively. I realize I'm not this great wonder in the earth who is living a flawless life. I live my best at the time, all the while knowing God is perfecting those things that concern me. (Psalm138:8) I see well thought-out plans fall apart. I see bad timing, missed opportunities and acts of disobedience. I see the consequences of my decisions – good and bad. I note my strengths and weaknesses. I see where I did not take heed to wise counsel and the results thereof. I also glean from right decisions and timely actions resulting in successful outcomes. Then I look at my emotional responses and how they left me. Oh, there is one other major observation – how I interacted with various personality types.

The outcome of this time of reflection helps me to better navigate my present to ensure a better outcome in the future. Life is a lesson learned. I'm the better for it.

> *"Life is 10% what happens to you and 90% how you react to it."*
> (Chuck Swindoll, Pastor, Author)

I want to leave you with a statement from Nelson Mandela (Former President of South Africa). His life was dedicated to confronting the gross social injustices against his people. His journey leading up to becoming the President of South Africa depicts the harsh realities and challenges he faced in the midst of tremendous opposition.

Your journey may not be that of a freedom fighter. However, you must overcome the challenges on your journey in order to embrace genuine freedom. Keep walking. Keep moving. With each step there is progress. You're not at the end of your journey yet.

> *"I have walked that long road to freedom. I have tried not to falter; I have made missteps along the way. But I have discovered the secret that after climbing a great hill, one only finds that there are many more hills to climb. I have taken a moment here to rest, to steal a view of the glorious vista that surrounds me, to look back on the distance I have come. But I can only rest for a moment, for with freedom comes responsibilities, and I dare not linger, for my long walk is not ended."*

OTHER BOOKS BY THIS AUTHOR

www.ingramcontent.com/pod-product-compliance
Lightning Source LLC
LaVergne TN
LVHW052256070426
835507LV00035B/2963